Conversations on/for Sout.

Narrating Nations, Performing Politics

A Conversation with Vasudha Dalmia

Conversations on/for South Asia Series Editors:

Sasanka Perera

Ravi Kumar

Dev Nath Pathak

Bio-note on the editor:

Dr. Dev Nath Pathak is currently a senior Assistant Professor and teaches Sociology at South Asian University, New Delhi (India) since 2011. He has a doctorate in Sociology from Jawaharlal Nehru University and his research interest consists broadly of cultural performances, art, music, and popular cinema in the region of South Asia. He has taught in the past at Jamia Millia Islamia, Hindu College and Kamala Nehru College of Delhi University, and at the Centre for Culture, Media and Governance. He has contributed articles to various journals and is Reviews Editor and Editorial Member of the journal *Society and Culture in South Asia*. Some of his recent publications include, *Culture and Politics in South Asia: Performative Communication* (2017), *Another South Asia* (2017), *Intersections of Art, Sociology and Art History* (2016). His publications are available at academia.edu.

Titles in the Series

Debating the Ancient and Present: A Conversation with Romila Thapar, edited by Sasanka Perera, 2015

Intersections in Sociology, Art and Art History: A Conversation with Parul Dave-Mukherji, edited by Dev Nath Pathak, 2016

The Question of South Asia—Reflections, Rhetoric and the Idea of a University: A Conversation with Imtiaz Ahmad, edited by Ravi Kumar (Forthcoming)

Culture and Politics of Nomadic Bantering: A Conversation with Shiv Visvanathan, edited by Dev Nath Pathak (Forthcoming)

Violence and Non-Violence: A Conversation with Faisal Devji, edited by Ankur Dutta (Forthcoming)

Conversations on/for South Asia

Narrating Nations, Performing Politics

A Conversation with Vasudha Dalmia

Edited by
Dev Nath Pathak

SAU SOUTH ASIAN UNIVERSITY
Sociology@SAU

AAKAR

Narrating Nations, Performing Politics: A Conversation with Vasudha Dalmia
Edited by Dev Nath Pathak

First Published 2017

ISBN 978-93-5002-553-6

Published by
AAKAR BOOKS
28 E Pocket IV, Mayur Vihar Phase I
Delhi 110 091 India
Phones: 011 2279 5505, 2279 5641
Email: aakarbooks@gmail.com

In association with
Department of Sociology
Faculty of Social Sciences
South Asian University
Akbar Bhavan, Chanakyapuri,
New Delhi 110 021, India
Email: sociology@soc.sau.ac.in

Printed at
D.K. Fine Art Press, Delhi 110 052

Contents

Series Note: Conversations on/for South Asia 7

Preface and Acknowledgements 9

Introduction: A Short Note on Ifs and Buts 13

The Conversation 29

Series Note

Conversations on/for South Asia

The Department of Sociology at South Asian University was established in 2011 within the Faculty of Social Sciences. In defining its vision and approach to teaching and research, the Department of Sociology notes on its website that it is "acutely aware of the non-existence of regular and serious forums for South Asian scholarship in social sciences to showcase our own research and thinking." This series is an effort on the part of the Department to create a platform of critical knowledge on issues that have been vital to South Asia.

As a series, *Conversations on/for South Asia* intends to keep itself open-ended, more so keeping in mind the necessity of inventing and re-inventing scholarship in and around ever dynamic South Asian societies. The series will not only publish conversations with South Asian scholars on vital issues of concern but will also be open to publishing other kinds of texts that contribute to a critical understanding of the region whose definition, intellectually, is mired in numerous debates and anxieties. It is one of the textual tools through which the Department of Sociology hopes to expand its thinking to the wider public domain in South Asia and the world in addition to its journal, *Society and Culture in South Asia*.

Each instalment will be published under the editorial responsibility of one of the editors in the series.

Preface and Acknowledgments

Narrating Nations, Performing Politics: A Conversation with Vasudha Dalmia is the third, following *Debating the Ancient and Present: A Conversation with Romila Thapar*, and *Intersections of Art, Sociology and Art History: A Conversation with Parul Dave-Mukherji*, in the publication series, *Conversations on/for South Asia* launched by the Department of Sociology at South Asian University in 2015. This is based on the conversation which was organized by the Deparment of Sociology on 27 November 2015 at the Akbar Bhavan campus of South Asian University. The process that entailed preparation towards this conversation was the same as the previous conversations in this series. It meant inviting the questions in advance, arranging them thematically, and executing the conversation. The questions were in the light of some of Prof. Vasudha Dalmia's publications, although not in a restricted sense. The details of these publications can be accessed at http://sseas.berkeley.edu/people/faculty/vasudha-dalmia.

Being at a young Department of Sociology at the newly founded South Asian University, we have grappled with the question about the nature and scope of our discipline and its subject matter extensively. We have noted on the deadlock of the disciplinary boundaries reflected in the selection of themes, concepts, and theories in researches and teaching. In the ongoing pursuit as a collective of sociologists and social anthropologists, we tend to ask: what sociology and social anthropology means to us given a qualitative distinction of our institutional location? Coupled with the institutional location, we are also aware of the qualitative distinction of our intellectual orientation. It indeed aids in approaching the question of disciplinary boundaries with optimum reflexivity. We thus encounter evident intersections between sociology and social anthropology with various other fields of enquiries. This conversation reflects our ongoing pursuits as the diverse disciplinary interests unfold at once and persuade us to enquire and engage, imagine and innovate, and dare to reframe our questions. And while this happens, we witness the possibility of making our disciplinary practices within sociology and anthropology more nuanced than the monolithic entities in the conventional set ups.

My colleagues in the Department of Sociology ought to be acknowledged for keeping such a pursuit alive and promising. I also need to thank them for making a conscious effort to steward the paradigm of intellectual and academic progress intricately linked with the institutional progress of the Department of Sociology. Various propositions emerging from the meetings of the Department have explicitly stressed the relation of individual and institutional in most of our academic and extra-academic activities. The Conversation Programme of the Department is one of the manifest examples among various others. Our endeavours, perhaps adding to the intellectual progress of individual members, also entail the entire Departmental collective. This is crucial at a time characterized by the reduction of academic pursuits into an atomized phenomenon wherein colleagues cannot be anything other than cold competitors. The spirit of conversation is indeed a good antidote to the prevalent anomaly that forges friendship, irrespective of the hard-hitting disagreements typical of the conversations.

Narrating Nations, Performing Politics—the thematic mainstay of the Conversation with Vasudha Dalmia—is one of the interest areas for some of us in the Department. The Department co-convened a conference on the idea of performative commmunication in the South Asian context in the past. Our young scholars have been interested in the issue as they debate some of these aspects in the M.Phil. optional courses. The ongoing interest highlights the imperative to construe the coming together of performance and power, culture and politics, which have been somewhat sidelined fields in the ambit of sociology in South Asia. Our interest in the cultural history approach made it inevitable to be host and participant in this conversation that was aptly moderated by R. Mahalakshmi who is known for her fascinating discussions on the various episodes of cultural history. I thank her for undertaking it with utmost enthusiasm. I must also extend my gratitude to my colleagues for engendering a consensus about the pursuits of such intersections, a tangible anchor through misleading fogginess about inter-disciplinarity or its many cognates.

This conversation with Prof. Dalmia, located in the above scheme, is a humble contribution on the explorations of the themes in religion and politics, culture and power, literary and manipulative inter alia. I must acknowledge Prof. Dalmia's deeper interest in the idea of this conversation, its execution, and finally in the publication of the conversation. She affirmed our faith that the disciplinary boundaries are not too tight to prevent dialogues. Needless to say, the vast corpus of scholarship to the credit of Prof. Dalmia has always informed and stimulated us in our teaching programmes and research.

This conversation like on the previous occasions was coordinated and organized by our students with dynamic interest. I thank Ratan Kumar Roy, Apoorva Kaul, Sandhya

A.S. amd Sabri Girisan for their active role. Many other students who were part of the students' collective, Rickshaw, under the Department of Sociology, came along to stand by their comrades in action. I thank them all. I must acknowledge the role of the staff of the office of the Faculty of Social Sciences, namely Samson George, Aman Kumar, and Jyoti Chawla. The credit for successful logistical arrangement behind our events is entirely of the FSS staffers.

In formulating the text for publishing, we have edited it in consultation with Prof. Dalmia, keeping the spirit, the feel and the nuances of the conversation intact. The mansucript has gone through grinding editorial reading, peer-reviews, and reworking. I am grateful to Prof. Dalmia for taking time off from her hectic schedule and reading and correcting the manuscript. I wish to acknowledge the significant role of Prof. Sasanka Perera in shaping the introductory outline. A critical reading of the manuscipt by Dr. Ravi Kumar helped in the accessibility of the text.

Last but not the least, I sincerely acknowledge and appreciate the creative efforts of Anoli Perera, a noted contemporary visual artist from Sri Lanka, in designing the cover for the present instalment as well as for the series.

30 November 2017
New Delhi

Dev Nath Pathak
Department of Sociology
Faculty of Social Sciences
South Asian University

Introduction:
A Short Note on Ifs and Buts

What happens to cultural history at the cusp of intersecting religions and politics? How do various genres of expressions, such as literature, popular culture, theatre, cinema and performances inter alia, respond to the intersecting religious and political perspectives? One can recall various examples to deal with the questions related to cultural history, religion, politics, etc. It is worth recalling two instances, one from literature and the other from popular Hindi cinema, merely to indicate that there are many more which could lead us to discuss the issue, central to the conversation with Vasudha Dalmia.

These are the instances of Rabindranath Tagore's *Gora* (1909) and Yash Chopra's directorial (ad)venture, *Dharmaputra* (1961), divided by a considerable span of time, genres of expressions, levels of aesthetics due to difference of mediums. Needless to say, this is a dramatic leap from the *classical* Tagore to *popular* Chopra, lacking in a balanced and thorough presentation of the trajectory. But, this is done only for the convenience of this introductory note that seeks to establish the significance of intersecting religion, politics, and cultural history. What happens with Gora can perhaps happen with every and any Indian, or resident in South Asia, or perhaps anywhere in the world today. The contexts are not very different from the dramatic situation that we encounter around. After all, the Charlie Hebdo[1] attack rocked European claims about multiculturalism. And so did an endless array of incidents from *Gau-raksha* (protecting cows) to *Ghar Wapasi* (reconverting the converted) in India by shattering the textbook claims of unity-in-diversity. The various faces of violent nationalism along the lines of religious, ethnic, and political identification are available in the cultural landscape of South Asia. Turning it from sublime to ridiculous, we have witnessed the rise of 'banal nationalism'[2] that operate with mundane prerequisites while driven by socio-political ideologies. It manifests in the increasing size of the national flag without even an iota of the understanding of the chequered trajectory of the Indian national flag[3]. Besides, one fails to fathom whether the larger-than-life size of national flags can evoke more nationalist sentiment than, say for example, the handy-small-size plastic national flag that street children sell at the traffic posts during Republic day or Independence day. Likewise, the intrigue of the national anthem in the cinema halls before one indulges in the entertainment is a hard nut to crack. Despite having a sufficient sense of reverence for the mellifluous and poetic national anthem, it does not make sense to stand up to the animated national flag unfluttering to a clinically sung national anthem soaked in the poorly composed music. One

1. See http://www.bbc.com/news/world-europe-30708237
2. See Billig (1995).
3. The story of the becoming of the Indian national flag, which was simultaneously a process of unbecoming for someone like Mahatma Gandhi, is candidly told by Sadan Jha (2016) in a well-researched, lucid account. The entirety of the story can perhaps drive some sense among those who tend to be easily carried away and subscribe to the reduction of the national flag into banal symbolism.

recalls the days in the schools in the small towns where singing the national anthem without many techno-bureaucratic interventions and state-impostion endlessly enthralled us. This was much before the grotesque idea of planting a military tank on university campuses to ensure naitonalist veneration dawned upon the wisest of the decision-makers in the precincts of higher education. Our evocative patriotism enabling us to be critical and discerning citizens is indeed clouded by the bizarre banality of nationalism. While on one hand they appear as the butt of our ridicule, and we laugh at them helplessly while we experience the constrains and overridding impact of the banality. On the other hand, we witness the macabre killings, gory violence, and inhumane spectacles of politics of nationalism. The manifestation of Sinhala nationalism, from violent mobilization of the Buddhist monks to military aggression along ethnic lines, is now a well known experience. It has a performative face, from 'warzone tourism' to redefinition of nationalism[4]. It has performed the politics of segregating 'us' and 'them', participated by the ethnic Sinhala, anguished Tamil, and the teeming number of visiting tourists lustfully looking for the remains of Ram, Sita, Hanuman and of course Ravana. Curiously, the performance of Sinhala nationalism, at the interface of religion and politics, has spectacular manifestations as well as micro-management. It shows in the sites of worshipping, shrines and memorials, war-monuments, and also in everyday life of the citizens. The Sri Lankan artists have documented the experience of Sinhala nationalism in various ways loaded with anguished narration of nationalism[5]. These artistic narrations through an aesthetic lexicon speak volumes on nostalgia of Sinhala

4. See Perera (2016) and Seoighe (2017).
5. See Perera (2015).

civilizational consmopolitanism, ethnic fractures and assault of state machineries. The inexorable religio-political vulnerabilities in various parts of the region give rise to a self-reflective conversation that this booklet offers, and an engagement with the two instances in the following.

Many scholars have written about Tagore's *Gora* and have pointed out its significance in understanding the religio-cultural-racial psyche of masculine India, the Hindu Bharatvarsha of Gora, formally named Gaurmohan[6]. Gora, the protagonist in the Tagore novel, is an embodiment of the paradoxes of modern India, a heightened sense of purity and strong fear of pollution, awaiting a moment of catharsis. He grows up into a self-confident man venerating the idea of religio-racial superiority through which he imagines a *Hindu Bharatvarsha* (the Indian subcontinent with the dominance of the Hindus), and he passionately argues in defence of the exclusivist cultural-nationlism. At several junctures in the novel it seems that a moment of cultural catharsis riddled with majoritarian communal violence is in the making, and that there will be an explosion sooner or later in the unfolding story. This is feared to be an explosion which will iron out, though temporarily, Gora's ambiguities. One fears that it can permanently establish Gora as a racially-communally—and

6. Among others, Meenakshi Mukherjee's remark on *Gora* is valuable to recall. "Situated within the larger conflict between modernization and the Hindu tradition—inevitable in a British-occupied India where the educated class was simultaneously going through an exhilarating exposure to new intellectual horizons through English education and the humiliating experience of political subjugation—the novel nevertheless foregrounds other local tensions as well, relating to caste, class, and gender that further complicated the question of freedom and selfhood" (1997: ix).

nationally superior breed. And thus it would be a triumph of a divisive cultural nationalism. But, Gora is not the singular character despite his significance as a protagonist. The other characters in the story assume equally significant positions, and thus they constitute Gora's disposition. The genuine grandeur of the personalities such as the benevolent Paresh Babu and an enormous splendour of mother figure, Anandamoyi, ever willing to accommodate and reason with the passionate difference of Gora and Binoy, is a catch in the whole drama. While Gora's passionate and unrelenting perspective finds audience, it is Binoy who goes through "the eddies of conflicting ideologies without the benefit of a debating partner"[7]. So is the appearance of articulate young female characters' quests, such as Sucharita's calm curiosity about truth and falsehood. While there is an urge to critically engage with Gora's disposition, there is an explicit reservation about the reformist vision of the Brahmo Samaj too. While there is a tension between the pure roots and impure roots in the formation of subjectivities, there is patient audience given to each fragment. The distant catgeories such as nation, community, religion, language and culture are important. But so are the fellow actors and their emoting acts in the drama, and hence Gora cannot escape the challenge. He has to be reflective, there is no way out. And thus while he delivers a monologue, he has to be audience to the equally passionate monologue of the significant-others. It is this complexity in which Gora meets the moment of catharsis with a realization that his celebration of pure roots is defeated by impure roots. That he has Irish blood mixed with his ennobled sense of racial superiority, comes to underline the paradoxical coexistence of rancorous rhetoric and levelling realities.

---

7. Ibid.: xx.

A similar moment of catharsis occurs in *Dharmaputra*, a film based on the novel in Hindi by Acharya Chatursen[8]. The film was produced by B.R. Chopra and directed by Yash Chopra, both originally belonged to Lahore before the partition of India along communal lines. And this film, though an adapatation of the novel, seemed to communicate the subjectivities of many who encountered the communal backlash on the eve of independence. The film was also seen in continuum with the *Dhool Ka Phool* (Flower in Dust), of the Chopra brothers, which made a statement on secularism in Nehruvian India, epitomized in the song, *Neither a Hindu nor a Musalman, you are born of humans and you would be human alone*[9]. Set in British India, at the height of nationalist sentiments amid the ongoing freedom struggle, Dharmaputra is an epithet for a fanatic Hindu young man named Dilip in the film. But one can imagine it applicable for the teeming youths ready to shed their own blood, as well as others', for the honour of the imagined motherland. Actually Muslim by birth, Dilip is brought up by a Brahmin couple in a Hindu household due to the dramatic plot. Swayed by the scriptural readings, politically mediated cultural values in the nationalist framework, Dilip belives in, much like Gora, the purity of roots and impurity of routes. While the purity of roots is related to the Aryan qua Indian Hindus, the impure route is invariably associated with the Muslims. Dilip is a staunch supporter of the annihilation of Muslims in the Hindu Bharat, but there comes a moment

---

8. Acharya Chatursen is known for writing historical dramas in novels such as *Vaishali Ki Nagar Vadhu* (The Bride of Vaishali), *Somnath* and *Dharmaputra* among others.
9. In Hindi it was, *Tu Hindu banega na Musalman banega, Insan ki aulad hai insan banega.* The song was composed by the legendary poet and lyricist Sahir Ludhianvi.

that shakes the hallowed height. The Muslim mother who had given birth, and abandoned the child, is pulled back by maternal longing. However, she returns to find a fanatic Hindu man who leads the mob of encited Hindu men, committed to killing Muslims for what they call—*Akhand Bharat* (Undivided India). On the rampage, Dilip is prepared to thrash even his biological mother till he is told by his social father Amrit Rai that the Muslim woman was his mother. And the reaction of Dilip is, 'My mother'? A short aftermath of this catharsis shows an emasculated Dilip doubting the distinctions along communal lines.

The imperative of the modern nations to draw cartographic boundaries is a foregone conclusion. Each nation thus belongs to the delimited homeland, with clear boundaries sacrilized with the idea of sovereignty. But then, these boundaries do not stay at abstract cartographic scale alone. They seep into popular psyche, imagination, value-orientation, everyday life, and socio-political mobilizations. They reflect in the protagonists in *Gora* and *Dharmaputra* until a dramatically mediated catharsis aids in a creative collapse. The collapse can make a Gora or a Dharmaputra sit either way, with the violent affirmation of a divisive nationalism or a self-critical realization about the limits of the nationalistic identification. Often, as evidence abound show, a catharsis leads to more aggressive reaffirmation of the divisive nationalistic politics arising from cultural history fraught with vulnerabilities. The case of Sinhala Buddhist nationalism in Sri Lanka was mentioned earlier. It is not much different in Bangladesh though there has been another kind of ambiguity integral to Bangladeshi nationalism. The Liberation War was fought on the grounds of linguistic and cultural distinction in Bangladesh. It was a bid to obviate the communal differences of the Muslims, Hindus, Buddhists and others. However, the communal angle was never out of sight since the oppressor, the Pakistani army, was Muslim. In recent times, the resurgence of the Jamaat-e-Islami[10] in Bangladesh is (re)affirmation of the communally coloured nationalism of enigmatic nature. The Jamaat-e-Islami is known to have taken an anti-Liberation War stand and some of its earlier leaders have faced trial for conspiring with the Pakistani army against the Liberation War revolutionaries. The Shahbag[11] protest by the Bangladeshi youth demanding the death sentence for the war criminals was indeed an agitation against the Jamaat politics. Nevertheless, one cannot deny the stronghold of the Jamaat-e-Islami in contemporary Bangladesh. It was pointed out by Ramendu Majumdar, the cultural critique and theatre activist of Bangladesh, in a conversation at South Asian University[12] that the Awami League government too cannot ignore the Islamic pressure coming from the Jamaat. Hence, the incumbent government bows down every now and then under such pressure, and recently decided to remove the essays by the progressive thinkers of Bangladesh from the school textbooks. Amidst such a situation, the incidents of the bloggers being hacked to death[13] in the streets of Bangladesh testifies to the Bangladeshi Gora's desperate attempts to reclaim the land of religio-cultural superiority. In the same stretch of argumentative thinking, it is possible to make sense of the

---

10. For more, see https://www.efsas.org/publications/study-papers/jamaat-e-islami-in-bangladesh-past,-present-and-future.html
11. See Roy (2017).
12. This was a conversation with Ramendu Majumdar on "Theatre and Cultural Politics in Bangladesh", organized by Rickshaw, A Students' Collective, on 8 February 2017.
13. Of many reports, one can see https://www.theguardian.com/world/2016/apr/07/secular-activist-who-criticised-islamism-hacked-to-death-in-bangladesh

religio-political intolerance that plagues India and Pakistan in different ways. An epitome of such violent manifestation was when an unidentifiable assailant gunned down the renowned qawwali singer Amjad Sabri[14] famed for singing *bhar de jholi meri ya muhammad* (Muhammad, bless me, and let no one go back unheard). One heard an Islamic justification that singing is sacreligious in Islam and hence the brutal consequence. A scene in a popular film from Pakistan *Khuda Ke Liye*[15] (In the Name of God, directed by Shoaib Mansoor, 2007) comes in a flash which depicts the self-righteous Maulana ridiculing Nusrat Fateh Ali Khan, another internationally acclaimed qawwali singer, for indulging in the allegedly prohibited act of singing. The sacreligious is located even in the domain of rational thinking as much as in the popular culture. It was evident that the violent religio-political assertion mixed with the modern nationalistic sentiments can go awry to the extent it would not distinguish the victims. And therefore the mysterious murders of many rationalists, namely Narendra Dabholkar, Pansare, Kalburgi and recently a critically acclaimed journalist Gauri Lankesh, was not without a nationalist framework. It was nationalism of a certain kind, drunk on the imagined supremacy of a certain community, and blinded by the political clout of a certain ilk. Much before the recent spate of intolerance and murderous opposition to critical voices, we had encountered the vandals objecting to the critical works of arts, be it in cinema or modern theatre. The community clamour against Vijay Tendulkar's plays depicting the moral hypocrisy of upper caste middle class communities in India is still fresh in cultural history[16]. And

14. See a report in https://www.dawn.com/news/1266514
15. For more filmographic information, see http://www.imdb.com/title/tt1068956/
16. See Pathak and Chhatre (2017).

likewise, there have been various episodes of melodramatic ban-seeking of cultural vigilants, be it against films such as PK[17], or against Wendy Doniger's Hinduism book[18]. In short, every now and then, a Gora turns into a Godse, as it were, to find a kill in various guises.

The conversation with the noted cultural historian Vasudha Dalmia in the following is an unfolding of such a discursive terrain where questions breed questions even though a sense of understanding surface for further questioning. Nation(s) stand in the dock and the legislators are grilled for explanations. Dramatics of national identity formation become available for questioning, and allegiances to the sources of identification are revisited with due scepticism. The conversation with Vasudha Dalmia brings about a realization on the significance of cultural history in the politics of religion, language and literature, identities, etc. And this realization is not free from the helplessness of a Gora, ever vulnerable to walk along with the provocations.

By the way of modestly presenting a background to this conversation, there will be an attempt in the following to flag some of the key aspects characterizing modern nationalities in the region of South Asia in general and the Indian subcontinent in particular. Far from the requisite exhaustive literature review, the attempt is to only underline the issues, which inform the conversation.

Synopsis of the Discursive Backdrop

Perhaps, the meta-concept of modernity is unavoidable in this wake even though there has been a sense of tiredness

17. See http://www.thehindu.com/entertainment/sc-to-hear-plea-to-ban-pk/article6314137.ece
18. See http://articles.chicagotribune.com/2014-02-13/news/chi-india-book-ban-wendy-doniger-20140213_1_penguin-group-hinduism-chicago-scholar

with its pervasive nature. Avoiding the much trodden conceptual trajectory of modernity, leading to the whirlwinds of post-coloniality, it is curious to cursorily glance at the characterization of modernity. If it meant a linear imagination of history and polity in the dominant scheme of reasoning, it meant a bewildering mish mashing at the concrete ground of experiences and practices too. It showed a tendency to sweep the 'stranger' under the carpet (Bauman 1991), while it also facilitated a creative ambivalence in which an unresolved tension of binaries unfolded (Pathak 1998). Broadly, this refers to the ambivalent nature of modernity, be it in Europe where the attempts were made to hide the stranger, or in the erstwhile colonies where strangers were too many to be tamed. In the Indian context modernism may not have always led to a negation of tradition and there has been a process of 'assimilation and syncretism' (Ibid.: 31). Intellectuals with reformist zeal such as Raja Rammohun Roy were born out of a cultural encounter between Western and Indian values. This is peculiarly an experience in post-colonial societies in the region of South Asia in which tradition and modernity, sources of enchantment and disenchantment, coalesce. The confrontation of binaries is replaced by a convenient suspension of tension by using the divide of public and private. Just imagine, with Srinivas (1971), the bulldozer driver of Rampura. He rode on the bulldozer, which belonged to the government, serving the modern needs of tarmac communication, repaired the giant vehicle whenever a snag occurred. He wore a traditional religious outlook, and to top it all he practised black magic for his clientele in his off-duty hours at home. The Rampura driver would be operating with the tools of technologically enabling modernity in the public space while in the private space at home he would indulge in everything from religio-spiritual to magical practices. This is not to suggest any cultural schizophrenia, be it in the historical-anthropological past (Pathak 1998) or in the sociological present (Deshpande 2003). But there is always a possibility of catharsis, which can take any turn, Gora-turn or Dharmaputra-turn, or a turn that can unceremoniously tender genocide and massacre replete in the cultural history of South Asia.

Engaging with such dual possibility, an argument emerged proposing the existence of the modern nation amid its fragments (Chatterjee 1994). Anti-colonial nationalism, among other things, resulted in a division that defined political liberalism too. There was a formal outside, away from private qua home, such as economy, science and administration. This was the domain where the West, the colonial masters, had proven superiority. On the other side, there was the inner, the spiritual that the masters sought to obscure. The inner, spiritual domain consisted of language, drama, novels, art, school and family inter alia. Through them, the modern nation sought to avenge the insult that it received in the outer domain. The ground of strength however becomes a foster-ground for divisive politics. Perhaps, the degenerate character of inner, in time to come, only showed the intertwined nature of inside and outside, spiritual and material. It amounted to suggesting that post-colonial societies were inherently, and spiritually, violent and divisive. This finds more acute expression as we turn to, for example, Hansen's (1999) description of the saffron wave, the ride of political Hindutva in India. Unlike others, who saw it merely as a political work, or a fall back to older tenets of culture, Hansen considers the rise of Hindu nationalism due to larger public culture. The Hindu nationalists used the public culture, practices and propaganda, to transform political Hinduism into a 'disciplined national culture'[19].

19. Hansen 1999: 4.

Needless to say, the idea of pure roots in the superior glorious Hindu past constituted the ideological apparatus. Hansen shoots down the perception that education, literacy and economic prosperity diminish the chances of ethnic majoritarianism. Instead, the formation of the middle class is imperative in the 'plebeianization' or 'vernacularization'[20] of the dominant ideology. While Hansen presents one side of the tale, a more sympathetic view emerges from another type of reasoning that highlights the idea of the colonized 'talking back' (Bhattacharya 2011). The commencement of the process of documenting history in colonial and post-colonial South Asia is an important marker in the 19th century. It yielded a parallel discourse on civilization, refuting the colonial thesis of the civilization mission and valorizing India's ancient Hindu civilization. Thinkers like Gandhi, Tagore and even Nehru expressly justified the need to insulate 'our' civilization from 'theirs' in various ways. This historical dawn of civilizational discourse however stressed the 'Indian' civilization and not that of the 'Hindu civilization'. Syncretism rather than exclusivism rode high in this discourse. And simultaneously, despite valorization, there was constant contestation about the degenerate remains of the past. Tagore and Gandhi, in their respective ruminations, made it amply clear that rediscovery of the lost glory does not mean an unreflective revivalism. And hence, while there was patriotism there was perpetual anxiety about cultural nationalism among some of these thinkers of modern India. It is safe to say, therefore, that Jawaharlal Nehru's discovery of India upheld a future for an independent nation, and not past.

This does not mean that manifold nationalism did not occupy the historical arena of performance. Vasudha Dalmia

20. Ibid., p. 8.

has vividly documented and discussed the language and literary politics, and it informs this conversation too. One can, likewise, recall King's (1994) description of tensions between Hindi and Urdu in British India, giving rise to two distinct senses of nationalism, of Hindus and Muslims. Hindi becoming a rival of Urdu meant a context for the cultural-national rivalry between the community of Hindi-speaking and Urdu-speaking populace. Hindi also swallowed other local languages, such as its rustic avatar Khari Boli, Braj Bhasha, and relegated many languages as mere dialects. In other words, there are ample evidences of the cultural assimilations in modern India undermining pluralism.

The discursive trope in the backdrop of this conversation is indeed too vast and any attempt to peruse it adequately in the limited space of this essay may not suffice. Nonetheless, the brief note helps in situating the issues which are recurrent, as questions and anxiety, in this conversation.

Conversation: Questions on Questions

The above is a broad backdrop of the conversation[21] organized by the students' body Rickshaw, at the Department of Sociology, with Professor Emeritus Vasudha Dalmia who taught Hindi and Modern South Asian Studies at the University of California, Berkeley, and retired in 2014 as Professor of Hindi Studies at Yale. She has many books, authored and edited, to her credit. Besides, the most important is the relevance of her scholarship in a socio-political and academic milieu where freewheeling conversation is too much of an effort. The corpus of her

21. The conversation was organized on 27 November 2015, as part of an ongoing series of such conversations, some of which such as Perera (2015), Pathak (2016), have been available in the public domain, and many more are in the pipeline.

writing enables the readers to engage in a conversation on the issues of cultural nationalism, literary and language politics, cultural history of colonial and post-colonial socities, and most importantly, the interface of religion and politics. The conversation was moderated by R. Mahalakshmi who teaches history at the Centre for Historical Studies, Jawaharlal Nehru University. Her interests include evolution of state structures in the early medieval period in South India, Tamil influences in the early historical and early medieval Sri Lanka, interrogating gender and hierarchy in early India, growth and transformation of Brahmanical religious traditions and institutions in India's early medieval period. As on previous occasions, this conversation too had participants coming from across universities based in Delhi, reaffirming our faith. Dialogues shall prevail upon academic monologues.

REFERENCES

Bauman, Zygmunt. 1991. *Modernity and Ambivalence*. Polity: Cambridge.

Bhattacharya, Sabyasachi, 2011. *Talking Back: The Idea of Civilization in the Indian Nationalist Discourse*. Delhi: OUP.

Billig, Michael. 1995. *Banal Nationalism*. London: Sage.

Chatterjee, Partha. 1994. *The Nation and its Fragments: Colonial and Postcolonial Histories*. Delhi: OUP.

Deshpande, Satish. 2003. *Contemporary India: A Sociological View*. Delhi: Penguin.

Hansen, Thomas Blom. 1999 . *The Saffron Wave: Democracy and Hindu Nationalism in Modern India*. Delhi: OUP.

Jha, Sadan. 2016. *Reverence, Resistance and Politics of Seeing the Indian National Flag*. Delhi: Cambridge University Press.

King, Christopher R. 1994. *One Language Two Scripts: The Hindi Movement in 19th Century North India*. Delhi: OUP.

Mukherjee, Meenakshi. 1997. "Introduction". In Rabindranath Tagore, *Gora*, translated by Sujit Mukherjee. Delhi: Sahitya Akademi, pp. ix- xxiv.

Pathak, Avijit. 1998. *Indian Modernity: Contradictions, Paradoxes, and*

Possibilities. New Delhi: Gyan Publishing House, Reprinted in 2015, Delhi: Aakar.

Pathak, Dev Nath. 2016. *Intersections of Sociology, Art and Art History: A Conversation with Parul Dave-Mukherji.* Delhi: Aakar.

Pathak, Dev Nath and Chhatre, Avanti. 2017. "Conflicting Moralities of Indian Nation: Reasoning with Vijay Tendulkar's Theatre". In Dev Nath Pathak and Sasanka Perera edited. *Culture and Politics in South Asia: Performative Communication,* Delhi: Routledge, pp. 287-306.

Perera, Sasanka. 2015. *Debating the Ancient and Present: A Conversation with Romila Thapar.* Delhi: Aakar.

Perera, Sasanka. 2015. *Violence and the Burden of Memory: Remembrance and Erasure in Sinhala Consciousness.* Delhi: Orient Blackswan.

Perera, Sasanka. 2016. *Warzone Tourism in Sri Lanka: Tales from Darker Places in Paradise.* Delhi: Sage.

Roy, Ratan Kumar. 2017. " Performative Shahbag: Debating Culture and Politics of Youth in Contemporary Bangladesh". In Dev Nath Pathak and Sasanka Perera edited. *Culture and Politics in South Asia: Performative Communication,* Delhi: Routledge, pp. 253-270.

Seoighe, Rachel. 2017. Nationalistic Authorship and Resistance: Performative Politics in Post-War Northeastern Sri Lanka. In Dev Nath Pathak and Sasanka Perera edited. *Culture and Politics in South Asia: Performative Communication,* Delhi: Routledge, pp. 65-89.

Srinivas, M. N. 1971. *Social Change in Modern India.* Berkeley: University of California Press.

Tagore, Rabindranath. 1997. *Gora.* Translated by Sujit Mukherjee. Delhi: Sahitya Akademi.

The Conversation

R. Mahalakshmi: Before we begin, I would first like to congratulate the Department of Sociology and the students here in particular for coming up with this very innovative way of being and interacting with scholars. I think that in JNU this is something that we could well learn from. I am happy to be a part of this. Fortunately all of us are mostly acquainted with Prof. Vasudha Dalmia who is an extremely accomplished scholar; her work on Hinduism in particular is something that I have read with great enthusiasm and pleasure and have learnt a lot from her work on Bharatendu Harishchandra and the edited volumes on the Oriental constructions of Hinduism. Let me take this conversation forward by inviting the questions. The first is by Dev Pathak.

Dev Pathak: To explore the Indianness of modern Hindi theatre in India you have discussed the Orientalist construction/discovery of the classical tradition and past. The early phase of Hindi theatre hinged upon the Orientalist reconstructions befitting the ideology and utopia of dominant groups (including literary elites). The question is whether the classical traditions or 'past' belonged to 'India' alone? What was 'India' then? Was the past configured only in relation to the cartographic entity called India? Is it suitable to persist with this association between tradition, a much more fluid entity as A.K. Ramanujan taught, with a rigid modern cartographic enumeration called India? Is it not much needed in our time to liberate pasts, traditions, memories, history and such entities from the stratagem of nation? This question is primarily aimed at initiating a discourse on the regional (also called South Asian in a different scheme of reasoning) pasts, traditions, memories and histories. Could we correct our fallacy of 'national' (Indian) pasts/traditions/ history/civilization by letting 'regional' take over?

Vasudha Dalmia: There are many answers to such questions, I am going to attempt one. Because there are several thoughts at work here and let me see what I can do with them. Let's take the first entity India; now that is something one could write a book about, right? William Jones translated Kalidasa's *Shakuntala* into English in 1789, and he conjured up notions of an India with a classical past of courtly culture, of kings, of courtiers, sages and beautiful maidens. Jones was trained as a classicist. You have to remember that he had another India in mind different from the India of the East India Company, as well as from the India that we have today. Jones was trained as a classicist and a Persianist. When he arrived in India he became an avid Sanskritist. So he was going to take over Brahmanical clues. You have to remember that the Greeks had their own notion of India, a land full of wonders and miracles from at least the time of Alexander. The notions Jones and his kind brought with him coalesced with notions that had circulated in the subcontinent, of Mughal Hindustan, of Puranic Bharatvarsha. They were imaginaries, if you like; they had changing boundaries. Sometimes these terms were used only for the region north of the Vindhyas, sometimes they included the Deccan. But were these notions only ever cartographic? They were culturally and emotionally loaded. They had a range of associations, as they do today. And this is much before it became intimately linked with the idea of the nation. We could rid ourselves of them, though, I imagine only with great difficulty. But it is not clear to me what we would gain by substituting them with the notions that have to do with North American area studies, such as the notion of South Asia[22]. However, we can counter each conservative thrust to freeze tradition by subjecting it to closer scrutiny. So, we can't do away with nation, we can't do away with India. I mean, they are there. We can, of course, use an umbrella term like South Asia for the region, though we would of course be coining yet another entity that could also freeze with time. But as I said I am not quite sure what we gain by it. I will talk a little more about it later. Even in my scholarly work I have found it much more helpful to follow the processes by which these constructions came about rather than toy with the idea of doing away with them. Nations are formed, canons are formed, classics are created. Once they are out there they cannot be wished away. They become powerful historical entities in their own right. Shakuntala was the first play translated into modern Hindi and then we can look at as to what happened to the translations. It was firmly launched in the Indian canon, not only in theatre, in modern Hindi. It is a very beautiful play. Perhaps it is not surprising that it has acquired this status. As we all know, Romila Thapar has written a wonderful book where she looked at as to what happens to Shakuntala in the Mahabharata, compared with Kalidas's Shakuntala. There is a project afoot to look at all kinds of translations to see what they make of this play, and they will tell us the cultural history. So I think as scholars if

22. The Department of Sociology, South Asian University, organized an international seminar on the critical exploration of South Asia. A discussion note along this line is accessible here: https://www.academia.edu/13843857/Mooting_South_Asia_Utopias_and_Possibilities_beyond_Geo-political_Calculus (accessed on 6 May 2016).

we look at these constructions, if we deconstruct them, reconstruct them, we have much more to gain rather than to simply deny it.

R. Mahalakshmi: Thank you. We have a question by Satyanand Vatsa.

Satyanand Vatsa: The idea of the modern nation-state is based on the process of homogenization. How do you think the idea of homogenized Hindu identity is a product of political construction? Also how do you differentiate it from the creation of a common cultural identity of Hindu in the colonial era? Bernard Cohn in his work *Colonialism and its Forms of Knowledge* talks about the development of civil laws in India and relates it with the process of knowledge creation. The concept of power and knowledge is intimately related to each other. Then, how are the theories of the absence of a common identity in Hinduism in the pre-colonial era not related to this process of power appropriation?

Vasudha Dalmia: You are saying that the concept of a common identity in Hinduism in the pre-colonial era wasn't homogenized. And how is the constructed identity created to power today? I ask you back: can it give us another kind of power if we de-homogenize? Let's look at this whole notion of homogenization and that's what I do in my answer. We know that the Indian nation-state was created as a secular entity. That the Indian Constitution took care to set up the basis of this creation. The terrible catastrophe of Partition, of course, did something to India. Pakistan was created as a Muslim state and by default India became a Hindu state, though it is not. Anyway, that's not what I am going to enter into. But, what did legislators do? We know that the Hindu Law Code of the late 1950s spoke of all Hindus. So, in a sense, our legislators regarded Hinduism as homogenized and all Hindus as more or less one people. And something is created there, just as it was created with colonial law because colonial legislators also regarded Hindus as a homogenized entity; it didn't differentiate. But the big question is, if we are speaking of religion, was Hinduism theologically ever homogeneous? As you may know, this is a question scholars of Hinduism have tussled with. It is very hard to counter something that has come into force legislatively. So we do have our work cut out. Modern thinkers have often sought to bring together Hinduism in modern India; we know Vivekananda did it with Advaita Vedanta; Advaita Vedanta is what offers itself most readily for this purpose. And we know of Dr. Radhakrishnan talking about a Hindu way of life as a shared culture. But in the past it was largely more in a political scheme in which oneness of Hindus and Hinduism surfaced. And we have to only think of Veer Savarkar who coined the modern phrase Hindutva and chose to view Hinduism as a homogenized entity. Perhaps, now also modernizing middle classes do that, who have a very dubious sense of what being Hindu means. Of course, those who have become communalized will look at it as a homogeneous system of belief and practices. So we tread on sensitive grounds as far as this issue is concerned, and we know people constantly get into trouble for questioning it. If we deny this homogenization, we are in trouble; this certainly has to do with power. But as scholars we need to traverse such grounds and deal with the issue. I see no other way, that we keep protesting, keep looking at differences within the ranks of Hinduism as well as within the ranks of other religions. Because they are not monoliths.

R. Mahalakshmi: May I interject on this issue of colonial constructs? It seems to be a misplaced idea to look at the colonial construction of Hinduism and to not see Hinduism as actually having a lineage in the pre-modern period. There are works that have been done on the Mughal period, for instance, on the Vijayanagara period which mention Krishnadevaraya presenting himself as a Hindu raja. In Mughal texts we have the 'farmans' (official edicts) talking about the Jains under the umbrella of Hindus. So we do have these very tantalizing kind of evidences that suggest that perhaps we are being a little too neat in this formulation that the construct that we have of Hinduism is something that happens only in colonial India.

Vasudha Dalmia: You know one thing that I always protest about—and that will also come up later—is that it's a colonial construct. Or it's a missionary construct. It's also a nationalist construct. I mean there are many collusive factors that are happening, particularly in the 19th century to bring this about. This kind of consolidation of a subcontinent-wide homogeneous, monolithic Hindu community—does that exist? That is a very general category which simply means non-Muslims and which can easily shape into inhabitants of Al-Hind or Hind. Now I know that it did crop up in the Vijayanagara period; that was a particularly sensitive time, which you will know much more about than I do, as also in certain Mughal documents if there is talk of Hindu, there is also talk of Hindustan. But that Hindustan is what Akbar talks about. He is not talking about a Hindustan which is the birthright of all Hindus. He is talking about the land west of the Indus and that is his empire including north of the Vindhayas also. So we have to look very carefully at how these terms are being used.

R. Mahalakshmi: You are absolutely right. Nowhere would one want to argue that we don't have a nation in the first place and we do not have that kind of a geographical entity called India but within a regional context there does seem to be at least an awareness of what could be an umbrella culture, or some kind of belonging, some kind of identity. I was looking at Ziegenbalg's genealogy of gods and goddesses in the Malabar region[23]. In the early 18th century, there were different kinds of gods and goddesses, who he placed within one frame. He perceives them as separate but he still placed them within one socio-religious frame. That is what I was wondering if we needed to interrogate. Hence, I do not disagree with you that a self-conscious identity is something that comes up at a later point of time but perhaps one also needs to see its source of inspiration.

Vasudha Dalmia: Well, as I said, there are several collusive factors in the 19th century which bring about a kind of a consolidation that we are still heirs to. But it ought to be noted that Ziegenbalg was a missionary and his propositions would have the missionary zeal and objective. Missionaries had a concept of, what Romila Thapar would call, Semitic religions. That's how they viewed the world, as consolidated forces just as they see Christianity as one, which they very well know is not one. Hindus and Muslims have been largely perceived in the same fashion, as two consolidated monoliths, that have always been pitted against each other.

R. Mahalakshmi: You are absolutely right. Moving on to the next question.

Abdul Matin: When you talk about South Asian literature, the 19th century plays a very important role in modern South Asia. How to interpret or read the literary texts of the 19th century in the present post-colonial context, where Bangladesh is a different country, Pakistan is different and so is India? And in the same vein how to define a category called South Asian literature? We can somehow have a South

23. For more on Ziegenbalg, it is useful to refer to Daniel Jeyaraj's *Genealogy of the South Indian Deities: An English Translation of Bartholomaus Ziegenbalg's Original German Manuscript with a Textual Analysis and Glossary*, published by Routledge Curzon (London) in 2015.

Asian University, but could we really have South Asian literature?

Vasudha Dalmia: It's a valid question. The 19th century texts—how do we look at them? There has been a veritable army of scholars, particularly in the West, who have in the last decade looked closely and analysed 19th century texts, particularly of the various literary traditions of the subcontinent. That's a very attractive proposition because these texts are easily available, they are in print, and particularly scholars in the West turn to English language texts because they have access to them and then of course we talk endlessly about the colonial presence and about how certain consolidations are taking place. Do we gain anything (from this background)? Let me take up the question by saying that we are South Asian rather than Nepali, Sinhalese, Tamil, Hindi, Marathi, Urdu. Perhaps, and we do gain in so far as we posit them as a collective related with each other and we don't talk about each as a discrete tradition (and we all know that they are also constructs). We are constantly dealing with constructs of one kind or another. They have close links and they are connected. But whatever we do, unless we do it critically, the matter remains vexed. However, so far we have to keep reminding ourselves if we look at it as South Asian as well as whatever the literary construct is, it helps us to bridge differences between Hindi and Urdu. Similarly, between Sri Lankan Tamil and an Indian Tamil (Sri Lanka), Hindu and Muslim Bengali (Bangladesh). Muslims get left out of Bengali literary histories. If we view them as South Asian we can more easily bring them together. Actually what we are talking about is a comparative project within South Asia wherein we don't just split up into departments/categories and we deem them interacting with each other. As discrete categories belonging to the departments of specialization they make little sense. I can't help stressing the difficulty and I will tell you why. We were once asked by Cambridge University Press to edit a volume on 'Indian Literature'. Goodness, how do you do that? Do you do it chronologically? Do you do it thematically? What do you include, what do you exclude? I asked my friend Francesca Orsini to help; we discussed it and realized that one could do this only at a juncture when we are entirely free from all other responsibilities. Such a mammoth task! It could be a fruitful project, but it ought to be recognized that nations are political entities. And our 19th century literatures help to create these political entities. If we write the history of a nation going back to a very ancient past we refer to literature. We have no other evidence/sources than works in literature. That's why the Vedas are so important. So I think as scholars what we can do when operating with these constructs is to look for the crux, to level critique, practise self-appraisal, catch ourselves out when we become part of this process of constructing ourselves. We constantly fall back to the same errors ourselves. It's a long answer to a short question. But with that we actually pinpoint the task we have as scholars, to constantly pull apart and then to bring it together again. Because we can't do away with the constructs.

R. Mahalakshmi: Yes, absolutely right; that sums it up very well. One cannot do away with the constructs, sometimes one has to negotiate with these constructs constantly. Sasanka Perera has a question.

Sasanka Perera: My question obviously comes from two kinds of lack of knowledge, I would say. But before I air my question, I shall mention that the word South Asia troubles me. At least in my department we really don't know what it means. It's very easy to set up South Asian University as opposed to understanding South Asian literature because you just need a piece of land and you put up a sign saying South Asian University, it's done. Whether it becomes South

Asian by just putting up a sign, is a completely different issue. For we are still imprisoned within the very restrictive imaginations of nation-states. This is why recently when we had a festival to celebrate the life and works of the poet Faiz Ahmad Faiz[24], we were not doing a Pakistan-India event. We were interested in whether his poetry was speaking to us across the region. But then, there were some voices from South Asian University itself which suggested "why don't you do it in Pakistan, why in India?" It shows that this category of 'South Asian' is highly problematic. My colleague (Dev Pathak) is editing a book which will try to look at the region emotionally in the way poets and others do. Now, to come to the question, as said earlier, based on my twofold ignorance: I don't know much about theatre, and I certainly don't know anything about Indian theatre. But I have been teaching a course on "Visual Art and Social Transformation in South Asia" and one of the issues that constantly come up in the course is a curious case. Art is seen as 'vehicles of social meaning' in the sense articulated by Cesar Grana which "both represent and realize 'the world'; and as a corollary can confirm (or deny) the stories of nationhood." When it comes to state systems of cultural reckoning in South Asia in general and in India in particular, can one argue that the kind of theatre which is supported by state structures is also understood in the same parochial sense? For instance, anything critical and politically conscious as 'foreign' and 'inauthentic,' and not worthy of support and so on? I have seen this to some extent in Bangladesh and I have very clearly

24. Department of Sociology at South Asian University organized the festival to celebrate the life and works of Faiz Ahmad Faiz on 26 November 2015 (http://www.sau.int/downloads/events/faizschedule.pdf). This was part of the consistent endeavour of the department to engage with literary icons and thinkers from the region of South Asia.

seen it in Sri Lanka. Does theatrical 'presentations without contradictions' (nationalist/authentic), a hegemonic discourse, prevail?

Vasudha Dalmia: I am afraid this is somewhat true. For instance, the National School of Drama, a centrally important institution for drama in India, took in a rather wholesale way to the so-called folk theatre. It connoted that it was the theatre which represented best (in terms of authenticity). But I suppose, once again, this is where we as scholars, and our students, our colleagues, the people we address, step in. And I have to cite once again with great admiration Romila Thapar who asked us to distinguish between state and government. Government runs the state; the government is however not the state. So keeping this distinction in mind and looking at our own recent past, we can say that governments appoint personnel as heads of libraries, museums, institutions and academies. We know that they play a major role in what is collected, exhibited, and under what heads they are exhibited. I mean the nature and scope of the focus that the Indus Valley Civilization got in the National Museum (based in Delhi, India)[25]. I would however like to think that this business about what is native and what is foreign, what is authentic and what is inauthentic, does not happen at all times. But there are periods when it becomes xenophobic and dangerous. We know about the book burning under the Nazis and the removal of experimental art works as distorted art, *Entartete Kunst*[26]. What has been happening in our country sometimes

25. See for details: http://www.nationalmuseumindia.gov.in/departments-pre-history.asp?lk=dp1
26. See for details: https://www.ushmm.org/information/exhibitions/online-features/collections-highlights/julien-bryan/nazi-germany-1937/1937-munich-exhibition-of-degenerate-art

comes dangerously close to that, doesn't it? Yet one can only hope it's a passing phase. That is also a part of our history that will also pass. They don't realize their own historicity, that's ironical.

R. Mahalakshmi: Yes, absolutely. Although, may I add as an aside that in Kerala *theyyam*[27] is part of the folk theatre. It's a ritual performance, but it's theatre as well. And we find in *theyyam* a lot of subversion. There is critique of caste by the lower caste against the upper caste. And in the name of ritual it reaches its climax where the conflict is resolved. The goddess comes and makes peace for everyone with everyone. Yes, *theyyam* does get state patronage, and simultaneously it is subversive.

Vasudha Dalmia: True, we can't condemn folk theatre sweepingly.

R. Mahalakshmi: The next question is from Prabudh Singh.

Prabudh Singh: In the light of growing Hindutva nationalism in India, what role can the imagined history of *Ganga-Jamuna tehzeeb* play to curb the resultant communal tensions? Did it ever exist in the romanticized form in which it is remembered today, and what is its present form, if there is any?

Vasudha Dalmia: True, nothing existed in the romanticized form, we know that. But that does not mean that Hinduism and Islam (I speak only of the two and not of Sikh, Jain, Christians since we mostly think of these two when we speak of *Ganga-Jamuni tehzeeb*) were two monoliths always hostile to each other. Let me tell you about my own experience. We do grow up in a very compartmentalized way unfortunately, most of us, if not all. When I was in the

27. See for detail: http://folkstudioin.blogspot.in/

University of California, Berkeley, Munis Faruqui was my neighbour. He was from Pakistan and he was our department's historian of South Asian Islam. In our conversations with each other, (and we had these on a regular basis) we realized that though we were neighbours in many ways we knew little of each other. We studied the same period (he studied the Mughal period and I studied the Bhakti period) as if they were two different periods. So we were neighbours in many ways. But we had very little knowledge of each other's areas of study, as we found out. It was truly as if we lived in two different worlds. So what were we going to do about it? We decided to remedy that. We held a conference have and we called it *Religious Interaction in Mughal India*. The proceedings of the conference have been edited and they came out last year[28]. There are good papers therein worth a perusal. Let me share with you a few of the things that I discovered in the process. The monoliths did not exist. Not in Hinduism, nor in Islam. That was absolutely true. There were multiple streams within each; sometimes clearly distinguished streams, sometimes with fuzzy boundaries. Politically speaking, the Mughal state could be different things at different times. So there was no generalizing; it could be patronizing, it could be persecuting, all this was possible. But what we did find was that there was always interaction at the top level between Rajput and Mughal and at the ground level between Bhakti and Sufi. Now, these are well-known facts; but we have to stop short of romanticizing them by stressing that Bhakti is Sufi, Sufi is Bhakti. It is not. So, we found there were many interactions. The compartmentalization that Munis Faruqui and I suffered from did not exist in the historical past. I can only talk with

28. *Religious Interactions in Mughal India*, co-edited by Vasudha Dalmia and Munis Faruqui was published by Oxford University Press in 2014.

relative security about the areas that I study. So what did I do? I looked at the Bhakti tradition, precisely the Othering practice in the *Vallabha Sampradaya*, one of the two most prominent *Vaishnava Sampradayas* or sects in the north of the Vindhyas. They had two compendia comprising the hagiographies of the devotees of the two founding gurus of their sampradaya, father and son, Vallabha and Vitthala respectively. I looked at their hagiographical compendium called *Chaurasi Vaishnavan ki Vrata*. This was the life stories of the eighty-four *Vaishnavas* who were the followers of *Vallabha*, the founder of the *sampradaya*. What did I find when they were Othering each other? Who did they 'other'? That was very interesting. Who is the other for the *sampradaya*, and why? Because they are very protective about their territory, especially newly founded *sampradayas*, they deemed other sects as rivals. They were most inimical to other Vaishnava formations, Shaivas, Shaktas, Brahmanical traditions, lower-caste traditions. There were so many others. And followers of Vallabha were quite vicious in denouncing them. Amongst these was also Islam. But there was no question of Othering the Muslim opposition alone, for the oppositions were many. The Other is the one that is most closely related to you, not the absolute Other, right?

R. Mahalakshmi: Thank you. The next question is from Apoorva.

Apoorva Kaul: That Hindi, India and Hinduism are colonial constructs is a knowledge limited to the intelligentsia. For people at large this legacy of 'Hindi, Hindu, Hindustan' almost seems timeless and organic. I was wondering what are the possible ways in which this myth of a homogeneous Hindu nation can be counteracted? Moreover, what role can literature, poetry and music play in this context in today's scenario where popular cinema too has nationalistic overtones? And in the same context, what happens when writers are brushed aside as troublemakers and dissent is considered merely symbolic? There is a tendency to label critical writers and intellectuals as elites far removed from reality.

Vasudha Dalmia: Apoorva, I picked up the first part of your question. To the large questions, I also don't have answers. We can only muddle it out together. And the first part of your proposition is that 'Hindi, Hindu, Hindustan, are part of a colonial legacy'. Let me take that one. I think we make it too easy for ourselves if we ascribe all construction to the colonial agency. The British may have viewed Hindus as a homogeneous entity and seen Hindi in the Nagari script primarily as the language of the Hindus. But, and we need to keep recalling that the linkage Hindu, Hindi, Hindustan, is based on a sense of territorial ownership and relation between religion and language was a home-grown affair. It's really not colonial. It was the work of nationalists and proto-nationalists and evolved in time. We see it in its germinal form in the late 19th century. My work on Bharatendu Harishchandra[29] and the consolidation of precisely such traditions (though Bharatendu was more catholic than some of his contemporaries) has shown that it happened in the Hindi heartland. Then I checked it up in my book who had used that phrase in the most pregnant way in the 19th century. It was a friend of Bharatendu's, Pratap Narayan Mishra who lived from 1856 to 1894. He expressed it in so many words. Now let's look at that carefully. He wrote a longer poem when he wound up his journal *Brahmin*. Such journals were usually short-lived, they were little magazines more or less and whoever had put his heart and soul into it were mostly men. It was actually always men. Pratap Narayan Mishra wrote

29. The work being referred to is *The Nationalization of Hindu Traditions: Bharatendu Harishchandra and Nineteenth Century Banaras* was published in 1997 by Oxford University Press.

this poem when his journal *Brahmin* was being wound up. He spelled out the cause on which he was working, and he asked others to carry on with the task. Let me quote a couple of lines in English translation to give you a sense of the kind of nationalism that he was propagating. I am translating from the Hindi verse:

"Those who don't know their own identity are like the living dead/so sing loud this grand mantra, Hindi, Hindu, Hindustan! Wise are those who don't discard their own language, food and clothing/in all true of good fortune Hindi, Hindu, Hindustan!"

Now, in its context it doesn't look too problematic to me and I will tell you why. Reading it a century and a half later (where another evolution has taken place) let me try to understand as to what he was saying. It sounds more as if all these self-identifications are being counterposed in a nationalist spirit. This is to distinguish themselves from the British, and not so much from Muslim and Urdu (though that can happen at any time I admit). It appeals to you not to give up your own language, own clothes, etc. It can be that I am being too charitable and seeing it really more as an anti-colonial than anti-Muslim stance. But, what I am stressing is that it's not a colonial construction at all. It is something that has come about. Where do you think it would still have its potency? It would only be in the Hindi heartland, not in all of India! And we know who the culprits would be, who would use it. But is it necessarily something that is accepted widely? You tell me. I haven't been back here long enough to discuss it in a really qualified way. But is it something that really exists outside conservative quarters also?

R. Mahalakshmi: Would anyone like to respond?

Audience: I'd say no, largely because many people nowadays are migrating out of their own homelands. I can speak of my family. My family members are staying all over India. And this might be true for most of the families, whether it be the migration of skilled labour or unskilled labour. There is also a kind of tendency to learn more about the outside world. And perhaps, this is greater as compared to earlier times. Thanks to the forces of job insecurity, or whatever that may be, now things have changed as people are more mobile for occupation.

R. Mahalakshmi: Would anyone else like to comment?

Audience: I don't think the divisive formulation of Hindi, Hindu, Hindustan exists beyond the realm, the Hindi heartland. But I do notice a new middle class, bred on the communality along the lines of Hindi, Hindu, Hindustan. Anybody from this middle class going to do a technical course/professional training or to do a job does not face any challenge to the divisive notion in their courses or even in their personal lives or in a political debate. So eventually what looks like a liberal middle class is actually very conservative in their thoughts and actions manifest in the cities or megacities like Bangalore, Hyderabad and other places. This is what is one of the causes for the rise of ultra nationalism in the city/urban spaces.

Vasudha Dalmia: Ultra nationalism, yes! But are they also concerned with Hindi, Hindu, Hindustan? Would this language combination be there outside the heartland?

Audience: I don't know much about it's status outside the heartland.

Santosh Kumar Singh: Not so much Hindi, but most certainly we can note the all-pervasiveness of Hindu and Hindustan! Coming from the Hindi heartland, educated at Jawaharlal Nehru University, and now teaching at Ambedkar University, I can safely say that Hindi has been very strategically subverted, silenced or muted but Hindu and

Hindustan assume a prominence. So, out of the three, 'Hindi, Hindu, Hindustan', Hindi has been sidelined. In any case, the middle class has a fascination for English. We know if from our experiences that when somebody's son or daughter arrives with the school report card and says that "I have not done well in Hindi." Our usual response is: "Oh, not a problem! How have you done in English or Maths? Fantastic! Then don't worry." This is the typical middle class Hindi heartland.

Vasudha Dalmia: But is Hindustan a concept also?

Santosh Kumar Singh: True, it is a concept of some kind. But if you look at the debate that happened recently in Parliament, the Home Minister of India asked that we should not use the word *dharma*, we should use *panth*. I said to myself, "Oh! This is amazing." This is not about some scholar making the distinction, this is Rajnath Singh, the minister with dubious credentials, trying to digress from the debate on secular politics by using another catchword. And I know there are people, such as this one in California who wrote *Religious Rebels of Punjab*[30] (forgetting his name) who have reflected on a similar distinction. This author in his work on religious rebels of Punjab stresses as to how *panth* is a better term instead of *dharma*. To respond to the initial question whether Hindustan is there despite Hindi been very strategically muted I would suggest that Hindustan is being revisited by the contemporary forces through new categories. Perhaps, through categorical distinctions such as *panth* and *dharma*, evading the questions of secularism in the face of

30. The author being alluded to is Mark Juergensmeyer who authored the book titled *Religious Rebels of Punjab: The Social Vision of the Untouchables* published by Ajanta Publications in 1989. A similar book by the same author titled *Religious Rebels in the Punjab: The Ad Dharm Challenge to Caste* was published by Navyana in 2011.

burgeoning communalism, the nationalist aspiration of pan-Indian Hinduism is prevalent. This leads to an uncomfortable version of Hindustan, more suitably a *Bharat* in the narrow perspective.

Audience: I think we need to check the significance of the usage such as Hindi, Hindu, Hindustan in relation to time and space. At the time Bharatendu used it in his writing, there was foreign oppression in India, as you have pointed out too. So, Hindi, Hindu, and Hindustan was an emotional response to the time. We also need to admit that writers contributing to Hindi literature articulated their critiques of colonial and socio-political oppression. In that scheme they invoked the term Hindu. For, the scholars of that time were searching for common threads binding the whole nation. So I think this not justified that we should look at this formulation from the perspective of contemporary time and space.

Audience: But the contemporary time and space are important. I was wondering how identities and languages play out. I attended a Catholic wedding recently, and the entire mass was conducted in English. There came a time when the Father (the priest) told all the non-Catholics that there was a particular ceremony non-Catholics could not attend. And, curiously enough, he instantly switched to Hindi as he said, *"Jo humare, Isaai nahin hain woh yahaan nahin aa sakte hain"* (The non-Catholics can't attend). I am just wondering if English is for Christians and Hindi would be for the rest of us.

R. Mahalakshmi: Well, I can think of Subramania Bharathi's poetry[31]. He often used Brahmanical motifs and

31. For more information on the life and works of Subramania Bharathi, this weblink may be useful: http://tamilelibrary.org/teli/barathi.html

deities to talk about nationalism. So it's not as if you do not have that kind of usage in other language-cultures. And hence, I think that it's not specifically Hindi, Hindu, Hindustan that ought to be deemed as the hegemonic idea. But since you are talking about common people I was wondering about my growing up in down South. I grew up in Hyderabad which has quite a cosmopolitan culture, and yet we didn't know too much about Hindi films or film actors. We knew of Hindi cinema music as *Binaca Geetmala*[32] used to be aired from Sri Lanka (before it came from All India Radio). But Hindi was actually quite far away. Whereas today if you go down South almost every child knows Shah Rukh Khan, Salman Khan, Aamir Khan, and other film stars. They are watching Hindi cinema and they may even be watching Hindi TV serials. So I do think there is a shift but does that necessarily translate as a consolidation of a certain narrow identity? I am not so sure about that because I think it's also true that you have a much richer public culture in the regional languages, at least in some of the regional languages that I know of. In Malayalam, for instance, we have wonderful programmes on TV and people sit down to watch those shows. This applies to Tamil and Bangla as well. So I presume there is no major shift but significant changes happening.

Vasudha Dalmia: But I think on the other hand what I am hearing is that this Hindi, Hindu, Hindustan is a thing of the past. It doesn't quite exist like earlier any more, except in some parts of the heartland. But Hindi is also not so important any more as Santosh Kumar pointed out. This complexity could be historicized and understood as having power and potency (let's say in a part of the 20th century). But what is

32. Browse for more information on *Binaca Geet Mala* aired by Radio Ceylon and subsequently by All India Radio: https://archive.org/details/RadioCylon-theHindiBroadcasting

interesting is that Hindi itself has diminished in stature. It's very diffused, from north to south, and yet not with a Hindi identity.

R. Mahalakshmi: Not so much a Hindi identity.

Vasudha Dalmia: Let me just reflect on the second part of the question, which asked whether music could be an influence, right? The answer can only be yes. I have a son who is an activist and who takes an interest in politics. I always fear for him because he is treading very close to the boundary. Music, literature of all kinds, can do wonderful work in countering monoliths. That's why poets, playwrights and writers are targeted, because it gets very powerful. Speaking of literature, which is my field, if it is multilayered it can be none other than critical. I am not only speaking of the known literary genres. I am also thinking of good journalism, of online blogs, of short features, of anecdotes, of letters to the editors. I read the papers very carefully (a couple of them) in order to understand what is going on. I don't see that the papers are toeing the line. I see actually that there is considerable opposition, quite a lot of response that may never die out.

R. Mahalakshmi: On that optimistic note, we move to the next question. This one is by Ektaa Jain.

Ektaa Jain: My question is about the attempts to rewrite or in fact actually overwrite historical narratives. This has always existed in Indian polity. So the critical examination of this overwriting becomes even more important when people actually learn through mediums which are somewhere motivated by particular agendas. Given such a scenario, what responsibility do you think theatre entails towards the audiences as well as vice-versa? As an extension of the same question, could performances be an alternative to the politically hijacked project of historiography and could theatre or cinema actually deliver alternate histories for different time periods?

Vasudha Dalmia: This is well linked with the music question that I responded to earlier. There is an attempt to hijack history/historiography. But have historians been entirely silenced? I hope not. It may happen eventually, but then they just go underground, don't they? They can't be wiped out, never have been. And then, when the times change, they surface again. I always have Romila Thapar in front of me. They have to tread carefully. Romila also says that. But have they been entirely silenced? There will be self-censorship, people will become more cautious, but I suppose we are still at an early stage where it hasn't entirely happened. We have lived through (some of us who are of a certain age) the Emergency[33]. What happens when people are persecuted, when things are banned, when people get into trouble and jailed, I am afraid also killed now? And if not killed that they go underground. They tend to be silenced for a while, but they can't be wiped out, they never have been. And when the times change they surface again. Indians are not, if I may generalize on behalf of the Indian people, endlessly tolerant of intolerance. Theatre and cinema have always played a role in providing counter narratives. Both are particularly emotionally charged, and effective media, with multiple possibilities of expression. However, if they get too explicit, they too are silenced, as we know.Art of any kind is a very powerful means. I just look back in history, in the 19th century, the Dramatic Performances Act, 1876 was promulgated by the colonial government. It is still in force. It came into being

33. For an interesting and revealing account on the Emergency in India, which was clamped on the country in 1975 and lasted till 1977, see Kuldip Nayar's *Emergency Retold* published by Konark Publishers (2013).

when theatre in Kolkata virtually exploded with plays that had *darpan* (mirror), in their titles.There were far too many such plays as though holding up a mirror to the power to be, to the colonial society and to the exploitation particularly of Muslims. Dinbandhu Mitra's *Nil Darpan* (published 1860) was the play about the Indigo planters' exploitation. This was the best known play of the period. As usual, critical expressions with effective outreach invite censorship. Because it is very powerful even if there are ten people watching a play. There is something powerful about a live performance. It may engender an immediate effect. So yes, it can provide a counter narrative, but only up to a point.

R. Mahalakshmi: Ektaa was referring more to the textbook kind of histories.

Ektaa Jain: I was talking about history textbooks and history books that cater to the performing arts, through theatre, cinema, all of them, because I think they also play an important role in projecting a particular kind of image of so-called nationalism, so-called Indian entity. They also create history.

R. Mahalakshmi: Why only history, they also create a sense of the society, polity and so on. Interesting, how you were speaking about history because I think somewhere one does need to separate the way in which the academic discipline of history works and the way in which histories are written, or talked about outside academia in non-academic mediums.

Ektaa Jain: My interest is more in histories outside academia, in the non-academic mediums. How people, a common person, might understand that very history through a different forum. For, not everybody would be approaching an academic kind of discussion about creating history.

Vasudha Dalmia: But, you know, there are always ways

of expression (and I suppose we need to look for them more and more) that can bypass censorship. And we have to aim for that. Because, nothing need be blatant that can be pounced upon. There are so many ways of doing it, particularly in any kind of a narrative form. There is so much one can do with the variety of narrative forms.

R. Mahalakshmi: In fact, during the Emergency in different parts of India, we had sharp reactions. In Tamil, there was Cho Ramaswamy[34] (who later on, of course, became quite right wing) wrote against Indira Gandhi. He scripted plays about Indra, the Lord of the Heavens, wherein all the other gods constantly berated Indra. The performance was abuzz with, "Indra you are such a fool". There was a subtext and everyone knew what that subtext was. So we did have people creatively reacting. But perhaps we don't have an emergency situation at the moment. And that could possibly be the reason why we don't see so much of a protest in that sense. But I think there are those little enclaves where things are happening.

The next question is by Santosh Kumar Singh who teaches at Ambedkar University, Delhi.

Santosh Kumar Singh: It's a privilege and so good to hear you because I teach a course called *Faith, Religion and Society* in my university and, of course, you figure very prominently in my course. I mentioned earlier the historian from California, Mark Juergensmeyer and his book *Religious Rebels in the Punjab,* and thereof distinction between *panth* and *dharma,* etc. I mentioned as to how the idea of secular is being undermined. My question is more about our anxiety today in India intruding all spheres. You worked on religion,

34. For a bibliographic survey see: http://www.goodreads.com/author/show/2817709.Cho_Ramaswamy

and looked at the terrain of theatre and folk traditions. Perhaps, you will respond to my anxiety. I am speaking from my own experiences in many places in Punjab and Uttarakhand, in Bihar and now in Delhi. I have seen in the *natak mandali* and *ram leela*, what you call, give and take. They were largely, very secular spaces of performance. The term secular has become too loaded today due to the forces trying to undermine it. I am sure you must have heard that committees have asked Muslims not to participate as Ram and Laxmans, the main divinity/characters in the performance of *ram lila*. Rather, they have been asked to perform the character of monkeys in *vanar senas*. Apart from the inherently racist underpinning of it, I wish you could reflect on the deeper socio-political crises. It is really frightening.

Vasudha Dalmia: You ask whether this is part of a larger design of majoritarian nationalism?

Santosh Kumar Singh: Yes, do you think there is a politics of a different kind being played? That's where I see the danger and not just in what we see every day on the national TV channels.

Vasudha Dalmia: The answer to that can only be yes. It is very disturbing.Such things narrow our own world and the scope for sharing. They are making our shared heritage partial, one-sided. It means ignoring talent, it means ignoring skills, and suitability, it means forgetting that Rahi Masoom Raza wrote the script of the famous TV serial Mahabharata. I mean, what more intimate linkage could there be between a Muslim and a Hindu text? The Mahabharata is shared, and we know it is in South East Asia, in Indonesia, and Muslims play the roles in the performance of the epics. We can't change the world with a narrow perspective glossing over the fact that our Bollywood stars are of Muslim origin. It is going to be interesting to see as to how the Aamir Khan controversy eventually pans out. He is too popular to be sidelined, as was Shah Rukh Khan. He is actually too critical a voice. These are disturbing trends indeed. But perhaps he can wend his way out of this and show us that there is hope yet.

R. Mahalakshmi: Ritu Sinha has a question.

Ritu Sinha: I am privileged to be here today in an interaction with you because I happened to have worked on Geeta Press in my doctoral research. I referred to your works and I must say it was very helpful throughout my narrative. Looking through the body of your works on Hindi, it reflects that Hindi adopted a rhetoric of Hindi, Hindu, Hindustan. You discussed it a while ago. But will you not agree that it came to represent all Hindus as it furthered the hierarchy and difference in newer forms? That it attempted to homogenize the middle classes and upper castes in north India? Will you not agree that a hierarchy of literary and non-literary emerged where non-literary Hindi productions were not considered suitable for the growth of the Hindi public sphere? If agreed, what could be an alternative picture of 'Hindi, Hindu, Hindustan' in contemporary India?

Vasudha Dalmia: I take up one aspect of this question, because we have already had the discussion on Hindi. A point of clarification: what do you mean by non-literary and literary works?

Ritu Sinha: Such as religious reproductions.

Vasudha Dalmia: You mean like the Geeta Press?

Ritu Sinha: Yes.

Vasudha Dalmia: Well, you may remember looking at Ramchandra Shukla's *Hindi Sahitya ka Itihas* (History of Hindi Literature)where he said explicitly (something that is practised in literary history) that religious works do not fall into the category of Hindi literature because they are not secular. Perhaps he made a wise decision. Just think of the misuse that could have been possible otherwise.

Ritu Sinha: In fact that is where my question is. When we look at the Geeta Press journal *Kalyan*, it happened to take up all the important genres which were coming up at that point of time in the larger Hindi literary productions. *Kalyan* was also flourishing with all kinds of genres to bring about the story of Hinduism. With its wider appeal, *Kalyan* was not taken as a religious journal. Many read it as literary, also to know history, through narrative (textual as well as visuals). If you go to Gorakhpur and remote areas of Uttar Pradesh you still see that people have a larger understanding of history, or of Hinduism, emerging from such kinds of texts, the local popular texts. They were mass produced and cheaply available. People did not understand what Hindi was coming from the journals. But people did understand whether *Kalyan* was talking about Hindi, Hindu, Hindustan. This is very pertinent when we talk about the Hindu public sphere. Those journals were important not only in terms of the content, but in terms of propagating the rhetoric on which Hindi itself was manifested in its so-called literary public sphere.

Vasudha Dalmia: I think you are right. Your work, or of Akshaya Mukul which you'd referred is showing actually the making of the Hindu world. And it is going to be an important work because it has been sidelined and it needs to be brought back into focus again because it was actually such a powerful force and it still is. Though not quite in the same way but it is also a disturbing force which Akshaya talks about. This question about Pakistan (which Sasanka Perera shared in the beginning) could be a Geeta Press question: "why Faiz here"? "You should go to Pakistan to celebrate Faiz." So it is a very problematic public sphere. You asked about an alternative to this Hindi, Hindu, Hindustan as I understand (perhaps I have understood it wrongly and so correct me). You equate Hindi, Hindu, Hindustan with Hindi literature at large? If so, let me take up that point because that somehow relates to the body of my work. I don't think that the vast body of Hindi literature took up the slogan Hindi, Hindu, Hindustan. I don't think they did it at all. Let me take the most famous writer (especially for the people who don't know Hindi literature) Premchand. Let me take one of his novels (that I have written about) *Seva Sadan*, written in 1916. It was published as *Bazaar-e-Husn* in Urdu. So it was a Urdu-Hindi work with which he shot into fame overnight, so to speak. It is the tale of Suman, a Brahmin girl, married, for lack of dowry to an impoverished elderly man, who shuts her out of the house in jealous rage when she comes back late from visiting a friend one evening. She is forced into prostitution, acquires fame as a beautiful and talented courtesan. However social reformers want to remove Suman, along with others from the courtesan quarters at the centre of town, and the Municipal Committee argues about the matter along communal lines: the Hindus see all courtesans as Muslim, the Muslims accuse Hindu merchants of profiting from their vicinity to their establishments in the city centre. Premchand shows up the artificially created communal tensions in the committee, he devotes several pages to it. I am giving you one example, there are many. Has Hindi literature unquestionably accepted the now-communal proposition contained in Hindi-Hindu-Hindustan? I don't think so. There will always be some who toe that line, but good writing, of which there is plenty, won't. So, there is no need to seek an alternative picture. We already have it.

As for the inclusion of expressly religious-ethical works into the corpus of Hindi literature, I would say that modern literature is secular by choice and by definition. Ramchandra

Shukla proclaimed as much in his Hindi *Sahitya ka Itihas* (History of Hindi Literature). However, he himself included the poetry of the Bhakti poets in his account, perhaps in his estimate this verse transcended its immediate purpose, became glisteningly beautiful as poetry. He reserved a specially high place for Tulsidas and his *Ramcharait Manas*, which is by all standards a beautiful work. As for modern poets and poetry, Maithili Sharan Gupt wrote his version of the Ramayana, the epic poem *Saket*, but it was not written as a devotional exercise. So, I would not say that religion is always and altogether excluded from the Hindi literary sphere. I would say, it is handled with caution. Some works are included; others are not. And in each case, we would have to ask, why this is so. And any scheme in writing literary history would have inclusion and exclusion.

Ritu Sinha: I referred to Dwivedi.[35]

Vasudha Dalmia: But even Dwivedi is more catholic than you would imagine. He is not a reactionary. A student of mine is working on Dwivedi and we have had many discussions on that. So Hindi literature, if it is good, and there is a lot of it, is absolutely critical of this position. Premchand shows up communalism in all his works. We just need to refer to *Seva Sadan* to understand. This was in 1916 that through literary recognition Premchand was showing the split in the municipal committee along communal lines and by showing it up he was critiquing communalism. He devotes several pages to that. The problem is we aren't studying Hindi literature any more. I don't want to offend anyone, but let

35. The book being referred to is, Hazari Prasad Dwivedi's *Hindi Sahitya Ki Bhoomika* (Role of Hindi Literature) which was originally published in the decade of the 1950s, later on republished by several publishers including Rajkamal Prakashan (Delhi) in 2008.

me put it this way, there are dysfunctional Hindi departments where studies in Hindi literature are no more a serious affair. Who looks at it critically, who works on it?

Ritu Sinha: I understand the tradition of Hindi because I come from a family where Hindi is read, my father being a Hindi literary person. I completely understand the position. I was talking about the undertones of Hindu nationalism which picked up during the formation of Hindi.

Vasudha Dalmia: Hindu nationalism is, by virtue of the very fact that it is Hindi nationalism, unfortunately is often implicitly anti-Muslim. But Hindi, Hindu, Hindustan is not part of Hindi literature, and that is good. There is a lot of good Hindi literature.

R. Mahalakshmi: Renny Thomas has a question.

Renny Thomas: As an anthropologist, I'm interested in the contemporaneity of politics of reading ancient texts. I am thinking about your article on Max Mueller which you wrote in 2003. I'm interested in knowing the contemporary political significance of Max Mueller's construction of the 'Aryans' as 'others', especially in the Indian context. I am asking this question because the present government is attempting to 'promote' Indology globally as a new form of 'international relations'. It is an interesting phase where the Indian government is telling the world that Indians are 'others', meaning Aryans. This is interesting in the sense that the present government finds its ideology and politics in old Indology, and wants to tell the world about the 'greatness' of Aryan Civilization. This version of Indianness excludes religious minorities and Dalits. I would be interested in knowing your views on the politics of Indology in our time.

Vasudha Dalmia: It's a large question. To make it short, what is Indology? I have to tell you my excitement when I myself read William Jones in the journal (or rather it was an annual number of *Asiatic Researches* that he edited).When I read his article about Sanskrit, Latin, Greek, Old Persian all being of the same family, I had sheer excitement about it. It seemed that the whole world was opening up. For the West it was a discovery and so was it perhaps in India. Because that's not how we looked at Sanskrit. It was an exciting discovery in its time. But we have to date Indology. Indology is not all things at all times. So in this early period, Indology was interested in a very close reading of Sanskrit texts of various periods.

In its earliest phase, Indology posited uncritically that linguistic families also translated into racial communities, that a shared linguistic tradition meant the kinship of those speaking the languages comprising it. The exciting discovery that Greek, Latin, Old Persian and Sanskrit belonged together led to some euphoria and hasty judgements. You and I are speaking English, that doesn't make us Anglo-Saxon. This is too obvious to be stated. In its early phase Indology looked at Vedic Sanskrit, and it's relationship to Greek mythology. But one should remember that Max Mueller in his later years distanced himself from his early racial beliefs. This is not often remembered. My essay on Max Mueller discusses him distancing himself from the Aryan theory of race. He perceived that it's wrong; you and I speak English, we are not Anglo-Saxon. So just to deduce race from speech is to take a short cut. Moreover, the discovery of Panini by the West led to the founding of the science of linguistics. Those were the only texts from the very earliest phase of the Sanskrit language. Mythology became a field to be explored. Looking closely at words and syntax led to the creation of dictionaries and grammars, there was work being done. These words and phrases had a cultural history, a ritual history, those could be written. Then they moved on to the Dharma Shastras, treatises on legal and civic codes, to the vexed question of caste, to the Puranas, to the insight that there were multiple Vaishnava, Shaiva, Shakta and other traditions, in the past and present, not to be subsumed under the head 'Hindu'. In fact there were many clearly and not so clearly defined streams within what we know as Hinduism today. So much work was done, is still being done. Given the present dispensation and its attitudes, you would think Indology was simply about the glorification of the Aryan past. This is the time for Indologists to speak up (not all of them live in ivory towers)and demystify, critique, and question. They shall not let simplistic notions prevail. It will also mean that we don't leave Indology to Western Indologists but bring it home. That we pay heed to what home grown Indologists/historians say, encourage more folks to study it. The mystique will disappear then, it will seem more like a science than sorcery. The problem is that we don't have a clue as to what Indology is. And perhaps those who are propagating it at a very high level also don't have a very clear sense of what Indology is. So they reduce it to the glories of the past. So what can we do against it? What have we done with Indology? Just as with Hindi which we have consigned to a lower lot of creation, we have pushed Indology to the West. Indologists are by definition Europeans and Americans. We don't often speak of Indian Indologists, though there are Indian Indologists, and some very reputed ones. I don't know whether Romila would call herself an Indologist but by all definitions she is. She is a historian and that's what good Indologists are. So what do we have to do? We have to bring Indology back; we have to do something about that. We have to engage with it so that we don't have a clichéd view of it, which we do and which our politicians do.

R. Mahalakshmi: I think that Prof. Thapar has recently talked about how we need to revisit categories like Indology. Because Indology ends up being a catch-all phrase for people. Moving on to the next question.

Ratan Kumar Roy: In the light of growing intolerance in South Asia we see that writers are often threatened and attacked by groups of activists for their literary expressions. For instance, in Bangladesh, Taslima Nasrin and Dr. Humayun Azad, who wrote on the communal culture and unmasked the image of Islamist extremism were targeted. After a decade, we are witnessing the murder of bloggers who are accused of writing about religion, culture, existence of God so and so forth. In this wake, when the Prime Minister of a country constantly asks us to maintain a limit on writing and to stop writing anything which may hurt religious sentiments, the question arises: is it possible for writers to limit their critical thinking and operate within the boundary while writing? Moreover, can he or she (writers) actually presume which words or ideas would hurt or humiliate any religious belief? So, what is your view regarding the expressions and literary exercise on religious debates and the intolerance?

Vasudha Dalmia: The unfortunate part of this exercise is the fact that those who say so easily that their religious sentiments are hurt—and they are not only Hindus, but also Muslims and Sikhs, as we know—themselves belong to the small handful of people who take it upon themselves to speak for whole communities. Their view of community is also rather distorted, don't you think? So what to do against it? We can only put our heads together and think about it together. The obvious answer would be to not allow them alone to speak, right? Now this is easier said than done, in that unpleasant moment of violence, few want to speak up. What progressive writer, thinker, blogger would want to call herself 'Hindu', 'Muslim' and so on? This is a very vexed question. To put the dilemma in a nutshell, can one be 'Hindu' and progressive?

I have seen that in various forms it does happen that people speak up, though largely as seculars. Though at this point in time, no one seems to be able to prevent that moment of extreme violence. And these anonymous killers and violators are let off easily, if and once they are located. I don't have any easy answers to that.

Some people make it into a part of their profession we all know that. That's what happened to Wendy Doniger's book[36]. It was one person, it was one person whose religious sentiments were hurt and why was there no counter voice, why was no one else speaking up? Can you tell me, I pose this question to you? Why does everyone else get silenced at once? Because it's so ugly? Who are these spokesmen?

Audience: It's not about the people. In the case of Wendy Doniger's book even before the trial the publisher decided to withdraw. We have however seen that even after the Hindu right groups objected to one of the history books by Sekhar Bandyopadhyay *From Plassey to Partition*[37]. They demanded that some portions of the book should be deleted, but the publisher refused to cower and the book stayed in the public domain. So it's more about the publisher's vested interest. There are many voices which are against this kind of politics of banning and burning. We see this on the TV debates where many people consider this as insane. Without reading any book how can you decry a book?

Vasudha Dalmia: You know that's an important point.

---

36. The controversial banning of Wendy Doniger's book titled *The Hindus: An Alternative History*, was published by Penguin (2010) and withdrawn after the Hindu unrest. Seehttp://www.firstpost.com/living/penguin-to-withdraw-wendy-donigers-controversial-book-the-hindus-1383581.html
37. Sekhar Bandyopadhyay's *From Plassey to Partition: A History of Modern India* was published by Orient Blackswan in 2004.

Perhaps we do need to bring it up in the context: how these discussions take place? Because those who protest will protest as seculars. They won't come back and say we are Hindus. That means that we are allowing a certain kind of fraternity to speak for Hindus, whereas the others remain mute.

R. Mahalakshmi: But it is a political position.

Vasudha Dalmia: The point is as to why have we allowed this term, Hindu, to be hijacked? I mean, has it become so pejorative for many of us that it can't be used by us? Is it that to be Hindu is to be like those who subscribe to violence? Something has happened to religion. That to speak as a Hindu would mean exposing yourself to danger.

R. Mahalakshmi: But that's precisely the point that one doesn't want to own up to only that kind of an identity. I am more than just a Hindu or a Muslim or Christian and so on. That I am more than being a woman, I am more than being a particular caste. So I think that there is politics behind that and I would strongly go with that politics.

Vasudha Dalmia: I don't know whether I want to speak as a Hindu either. But I just pose it as a theoretical question. How can we deny caste which we profit from? How can we deny being Hindu which we profit from in any communal situation? Effectively that's what we seculars are doing, aren't we? We are opting entirely out of it and we are leaving it to others (I know this is not a popular position Mahalaxmi). The point that I am making is that we have allowed actually a certain kind of thinking to hijack anything which has to do with religion. And that is very dangerous because only they will speak for us.

R. Mahalakshmi: I think that this debate can just go on.

Audience: I wonder whether there is a space in India for identifying oneself as Hindu or Muslim. I am not just talking about today's political regime. But haven't the scholars, say

Salman Rushdie, also faced this issue? Is there a space for critical thinking in India which is supported by law and order? Why is the Jaipur Literary Festival always reluctant to support and protect Salman Rushdie? Because the languages of a nation do not have to be mediated by any position. Because the notion of secularism itself is a very contested one in India. Because on one hand, there is one constitutional notion which says that we are all secular and even the Supreme Court upheld the constitutional position through the Bommai case/judgement. But on the other, there is a discrepancy between the Western and the Indian notion of secularism. So, whether secular or not (I think that itself is not the question), the issue is whether to promote critical thinking in India. Are we actually tolerant towards critical thinking at all? Being secular, being religious, being atheist, being a theist, all these are significant questions because there are no overriding meta-narratives (as we experienced while discussing Hindi, Hindu, Hindustan). Because I don't think Hinduism needs any meta-narrative. It doesn't need to be mediated through one particular language. Because there are so many preachers in Kannada. The critical thinking is really suppressed there. However let's take the case of the recent murder of Prof. Kalburgi[38]. So the question is not about the tension between secularism versus nationalism, or religion versus any other non-theological position. I think there is a problem with critical thinking in India itself. It is a fundamental epistemic question.

Vasudha Dalmia: That's a very important point.

R. Mahalakshmi: I think that one should allow for spaces on all sides.

---

38. See for more: http://www.thehindu.com/news/national/karnataka/kannada-writer-mm-kalburgi-shot-dead/article7596386.ece

Vasudha Dalmia: Placing yourself on the right side, the politically correct side, by saying you are secular?

Audience: I shall make a short comment. I think somewhere the question is regarding the freedom of writing, and how that gets constrained. Politics of censorship, which we were discussing a while back, has undercurrents. And hence we notice the partisan character of censorship: What is censored and what is not censored? For example, we have the documentary film *India's Daughter*[39] which was online for a day and after a day it got censored. Afterwards, the news channels were showing only excerpts of the documentary, a curtailed sense of the entire documentary. When the audience watched the entire documentary at one go the interpretation was different. This is how politically motivated censorship works.

Vasudha Dalmia: You know these questions which can be answered in one sentence, I will try to pass after counter-posing: is censorship necessary? The answer would obviously be—no! But what can we as scholars do about it? We can question it. We can discuss the issue at hand. In some way this is what I am trying to do so as to not confine myself to 'a yes or no answer'. I agree with you, of course.

R. Mahalakshmi: Avanti Chhatre has a question about political and performative structures.

---

39. The film which created unrest amongst the protesters in India is available here: https://www.youtube.com/watch?v=w3mRj0VoxOA. Though it was available on https://archive.org/details/BBCDocumentaryIndiasDaughterOnNirbhayaDelhiGangRapJyotiSingh, it does not seem to exist any more. A critical take on the film in the aftermath of controversy appeared here: http://www.newindianexpress.com/nation/Deception-Lies-Behind-Making-of-India%E2%80%99s-Daughter/2015/03/09/article2704869.ece.

Avanti Chhatre: It's actually a very naive question, but I am a student of sociology and I would like to study theatre, but I am told that this is not "sociology" and I should do something that is more "sociological". I am asked by folks in a university like Jawaharlal Nehru University as to "why don't you apply to the school of Arts and Aesthetics, or school of language and literature, to work on theatre?" What's your opinion on these disciplinary confines, these rigid boundaries? There can be no dialogue between these various disciplinary compartments.

Vasudha Dalmia: These are dogmas. I feel strongly about this because of my own intellectual trajectory. I am not quite sure to which discipline I belong. I have been classed as a historian, though I study literature, theatre and religion and I have held positions in these fields. I remember a historian friend asked me once (when my Bharatendu book had just appeared) that I should make up my mind, I should decide what I was. I had written a 100 pages on literature and he said, "why these 100 pages on literature, you are a historian?" I imagine that I am a cultural historian though it didn't occur to me to say that. No clear badge. But you know I hesitate to use the word interdisciplinary. It's used a lot; though dialogue across disciplines is fine. You know interdisciplinary can mean you are not committed to any discipline, you have training in no discipline. You are free to do what you like. It is obviously very productive to mix and match, to interrogate, to transgress. But in order to transgress, we need to be located somewhere, within some discipline or the other, and then you transgress. So if you are looking at theatre as a sociologist, my question to you would be (and I would like you to answer that): Is your way of looking at theatre different from theatre scholars? Are you aware of the difference?

Avanti Chhatre: I think as a sociologist I would be more interested in the socio-economic background against which theatre emerges.

Vasudha Dalmia: Right, so that's very good. So if you are very clear about what you are doing and how it is different and what you are bringing to it, what you contribute to it, then I think you are really performing a service to your discipline. I don't think anyone would stop you if you are very clear about what you are doing. Otherwise you become a persecuted minority.

R. Mahalakshmi: Curiously, Roma Chatterji and Vinay Kumar Srivastava (both anthropologists) come often as examiners of theses in our department (Centre for Historical Research). And they say that they don't get called by the Sociology Department in JNU as often! So, one does commit these transgressions. But I do agree with you that somewhere the methodology, the way in which a discipline works, the boundaries that it sets, is very important for us to train in.

The next couple of questions are by Dev Pathak.

Dev Pathak: You have echoed a lament on relatively 'depoliticized' contemporary theatre in India. It does appear true to an extent particularly when one looks at theatre in a comparative scheme and one finds the heydays of Indian People's Theatre Association (IPTA) more politically promising. But then, is there no politics in the relatively depoliticized theatre today? Is contemporary theatre really depoliticized? If yes, perhaps there is a need to debate the idea of political theatre. What is political and what is not in the wake of contemporary theatre in India? One also needs to interrogate the nature and scope of politics of IPTA, which has a fraught history with myriad twists and turns. Was a political IPTA the best ever model of political theatre? To make it more straight, does vending rhetoric alone qualify for political theatre?

Vasudha Dalmia: Proclamations alone don't make for political theatre, though we would have to agree what we mean by it. In a sense all theatre is political, it either takes a stand or it doesn't and in not taking it, it is also stating something. The politics of IPTA, as I recall, were stated quite clearly in 1943, the Association was anti-fascist, the Second World War was still raging, and anti-colonial, the 1942 Quit India movement, was fresh in everyone's memory. Let me focus on folk theatre, which I have written about at some length. The folk forms that IPTA sought to re-use had an express purpose, it was not only to bring a fresh wind to urban theatre; it was to carry a message, also to the rural areas in which IPTA performed. Was it the best ever model? No, it was one model, which belonged very much in its time. After independence, folk theatre continued to provide inspiration. We have only to think of that classic, Dharmavir Bharati's *Andha Yug* (1954). The very vital vibrant theatre of the 1960s and 1970s saw various uses of folk-traditional devices, quickened by the politics and practices of Brecht's epic theatre, as in Karnad's *Hayavadan* (1970) and Tendulkar's *Ghasiram Kotwal* (1972), we have only to think of the chorus of Brahmins. These were not formula plays. Were they political? In the widest sense, I think they were. But in the 1980s, with the culture of the Festivals of India, something else began to happen. Folk theatre became not only a commodity to be exported—Eternal India—but even in internal performances, it was reduced to a formula—folkloristic, decorative. It was exclusively patronized by the Sangeet Natak Akademi; exclusively performed by the National School of Drama Repertory. I have written about this at length in my book on theatre. Yes, it was political, in the sense that it was regressive, it harked back to some past, frozen in time, which was supposed to be pan-Indian, to hark back to our supposed roots, Suresh Awasthi coined the phrase, 'Theatre of roots'. But you are quite right to pull me up. Nothing is non-political. I was careless in my condemnation. I have also to get a better sense of what is happening in contemporary theatre, here in Delhi and elsewhere to make any pronouncements about theatre today. Some years ago, when I was on the selection committee of the National School of Drama for their annual Rang Mahotsav, their drama festival, I had occasion to see a range of plays. The theatre of the North East, perhaps not surprisingly, was very vibrant, very political, as also of Kerala: vital, imaginative scripts, choreography, performances.

Dev Pathak: In an insightful discussion you help us understand Jayashankar Prasad's reservation about Parsi theatre (for its commercial objectives); and you have elucidated that melodrama of Parsi theatre still surfaced in Prasad's dramaturgy. In this regard, it ought to be asked whether melodrama has not been an essential feature of the performative traditions in South Asia? Though, the regional variety of melodrama is not the same as it's European counterpart, and it could also not be reduced into Richard Schechner's scheme of Rasa-aesthetics. Nonetheless, there is a distinct sense of melodrama in various performances, much in tandem with heightened emotions in the ancient epics. Hence, what is so surprising if Hindi (nationalist) theatre too had it's own variety of melodrama? Besides, do you think melodrama could be an anchor to connect various forms of performances, be they termed folk, popular, cinematic, classical, etc., across time and space?

Vasudha Dalmia: Once again, you are right about melodrama, literally 'music-drama', with a very definite sense of right and wrong which generally triumph in the end. These are seen as the common denominating factors of melodrama, not only heightened emotions, though I would have to go into more detail about Prasad's historical play *Dhruvaswamini* (1933), in the context of which I talked about melodrama. It is meant to be a historical play, set in the Gupta period. What disservice does melodrama do to the play? *Dhruvaswamini* is a fiery play, a feminist play, radical for its times, where the leading women express their inner feelings, desires, where they take action or spur their hesitant men into action. It has a fine psychology—this is how life is, one thinks—somehow in that context the very obvious righting of wrongs strikes discord—this is not how life is, one thinks. But this reading can be a matter of opinion. Can melodrama be the anchor which can hold together "folk, popular, cinematic, classical, etc. across time and space?" If you mean can we use it as an analytic tool to read various manifestations of these genres, yes, why not? But we would have to agree about what we would gain by doing so, by shearing through all these forms with the same comb? Would we not be reducing them to sameness or have I understood you wrongly?

R. Mahalakshmi: And on that note we are going to wind up this session. I am sure you will agree with me that it's been a very fruitful session. We had more questions; I am very sorry for not taking those. But because the people who posted those questions had already asked questions, we thought that we will just limit it to this. I know that gastronomic considerations need to prevail at 1.15 pm and so on that happy note let's wind up. Thank you very much, Vasudha. Thank you once again to the Department of Sociology, the rickshawallahs and South Asian University.

Vasudha Dalmia: Thank you very much. It has been a rare opportunity to interact with students.